Beyond Green Belts

Managing Urban Growth in the 21st Century

also published by Jessica Kingsley Publishers
and the Regional Studies Association

Regional Policy at the Crossroads: European Perspectives
Edited by Louis Albrechts, Frank Moulaert, Peter Roberts
and Erik Swyngedouw
1989 220 pages ISBN 1 85302 021 4 hardback
ISBN 1 85302 024 9 paperback

Beyond Green Belts
Managing Urban Growth in the 21st Century

Jessica Kingsley Publishers *and*
The Regional Studies Association
London

First published in 1990 by
Jessica Kingsley Publishers Ltd
118 Pentonville Road
London N1 9JN
and
Regional Studies Association

Cover illustration by Christopher Ranger

British Library Cataloguing in Publication Data
Herington, John
   Beyond green belts
   1. Great Britain. Urban regions. Growth. Policies
   I. Title II. Regional Studies Association
   307'.14'0941

  ISBN 1-85302-055-9

Printed and bound in Great Britain by
Biddles Ltd, Guildford and King's Lynn

This report was written for the Regional Studies Association by John Herington. It reflects the majority views of the Working Party on Green Belts which was established by the Association in 1986. The terms of reference of the group were to undertake a general review of Green Belt policy in the United Kingdom with a view to evaluating the importance of Green Belts as a tool for urban and regional policy at the present time. Research papers were commissioned from individual members of the Working Party and formed the basis of the report. Particular thanks are due to all those who attended meetings at Loughborough University and contributed written material, especially David Evans who helped to complete sections of the report and compile a bibliography. David Morrison of the Scottish Development Department is also thanked for providing most useful summary data on Scotland's Green Belts.

Contributors to the Working Party

Tim Brown, School of Land and Building Studies, Leicester Polytechnic

Glyn Bryant, London Borough of Bexley

David Carter, Team Leader, Strategic Planning, Birmingham City Council

Steven Clark, Group Leader, Forward Planning, London Borough of Ealing

David Evans, Research Associate, Department of Geography, Loughborough University

Peter Gooding, Senior Planner, Department of Planning and Transportation, Nottinghamshire County Council

John Herington (co-ordinator), Senior Lecturer, Department of Geography, Loughborough University.

Steven Molnar, Centre for Urban and Regional Studies, Birmingham University; Hampshire County Council

Richard Mowbray, Department of Economics and Management, Paisley College of Technology

Tim Shaw, Department of Town and Country Planning, University of Newcastle upon Tyne

Ian Walters, Norfolk County Council

CONTENTS

1

The Historical Case for Green Belts

The role of England's Green Belts is defined in Planning Policy Guidance Note 2[1]: they check the unrestricted sprawl of large built-up areas, safeguard the surrounding countryside from further encroachment, prevent neighbouring towns from merging, preserve the special character of historic towns and assist in urban regeneration.

Green Belts also have an important secondary role in providing access to open countryside for recreation and outdoor leisure pursuits; this role is acknowledged in the latest government guidance for England (PPG 2, para 5). The five principal objectives are broader than the historical purposes of the Green Belt policy as enshrined in the Duncan Sandys Circular (Circular 42/55, which was followed by Circular 50/57) in one respect only - they emphasise the need to redirect urban growth inwards to assist urban regeneration. Within the Green Belts approval for the construction of new buildings or changes of use will be refused for purposes other than 'agriculture and forestry, outdoor sport, cemeteries, institutions standing in extensive grounds, or other uses appropriate to a rural area. '

In Scotland the objectives of Green Belt policy are set out in Circular 24/85, 'Development in the Countryside and Green Belts'.[2] The Scottish purposes are rather different, namely to maintain the identity of towns by establishing a clear definition of their physical boundaries and preventing coalescence; to provide countryside for recreation or institutional purposes of various kinds; and to maintain the landscape setting of towns. Permitted developments are 'agriculture, horticulture, woodland management and recreation, or establishments and institutions standing in extensive grounds (such as wooded policies or parkland) or other uses appropriate to the rural character of the area'. Thus in Scotland greater emphasis is given to the environmental purpose of Green Belts; provision for recreation is also included as a primary objective.

The Scottish Circular restates the earlier Department of Health Circular, but departs from the English approach in one important respect - the control of development in the Scottish countryside was seen to be linked to the protection of Green Belts (hence the title 'Development in the Countryside and Green Belts'). In England and Wales the government has issued general countryside development policy separately in the form of Circular 16/87, 'Development involving agricultural land'. As a result a much more integrated approach to the planning of Green Belt and non-Green Belt areas is achieved in Scotland.

The spatial distribution of Green Belts is uneven. While all conurbations have surrounding Green Belts, this is not true of all provincial cities, for example Hull, Leicester, Norwich, Cardiff and Dundee (see Appendix II) do not have Green Belts.

There are also some significant variations in the geographical coverage of Green Belts north and south of the border (see Appendices I and II). In 1988 Green Belts covered 1,821,862 hectares in England and Wales, approximately 12 per cent of total land area. This formulation is slightly misleading since there are, in fact, no Green Belts in Wales. In Scotland the approved Green Belts cover a total of 135,930 hectares or 1.72 per cent of the land area. The extent of designated Green Belt in England has risen substantially since 1979, while in Scotland it has been reduced to almost half the 1979 figure of 218,470 hectares. This is almost entirely accounted for by the scaling-down of the Green Belt proposed around Aberdeen and the abandonment of the Dundee Green Belt. (Grampian Regional Council argued that a very large area did not meet the spirit of Circular 24/85 and that other countryside policies would provide adequate protection. Dundee's case is discussed at the end of Chapter 2.)

THE BACKGROUND - PREWAR AND EARLY POSTWAR PROBLEMS

The origins of the Green Belt concept can be traced back as far as the sixteenth century but are more usually associated with Ebenezer Howard. In 1898, Howard proposed the idea of relatively narrow 'country belts' of permanently reserved open land to form a green backcloth to the urban centres. He was concerned about the growth and spread of large cities and proposed shaping a pattern of smaller satellite garden cities within the urban region. His green areas were not just 'stoppers' of potential sprawl, however, they created the opportunity for both food production and recreation, roles for the Green Belts which have always remained subsidiary to their protective function.

London was the first city to gain a Green Belt. Following the ideas of Sir Raymond Unwin for a 'green girdle', contained in the Greater London Regional Plan of 1933, the Greater London Regional Planning Committee adopted a policy to establish the Green Belt in 1935. Without planning controls they had to purchase land to ensure its protection. The London and Home Counties (Green Belt) Act 1938 enabled the purchase of 35,000 acres of land at a time of cheap land prices. Other large cities were also involved in land purchase (Sheffield, Manchester, Leeds). The largely negative controls contained in the 1947 Town and Country Planning Act provided the legal basis for the regulation of development and the compensation for loss of development value in Green Belts.

Regional differences were evident in the interpretation of the Green Belt concept. Sir Patrick Abercrombie established three objectives for the Green Belt defined in the Greater London Plan of 1944: restriction of urban growth, definition of an outer limit or boundary to restrictions, and provision of recreation as a primary use of the land. In contrast, Abercrombie's Clyde Valley Regional Plan of 1946 defined a less restrictive 'green setting' within which the expansion of several urban centres, Glasgow included, could be planned. The Green Belts around London and Glasgow were a response to pre-war and wartime conditions and were to prove to be blueprints for the Green Belt policies adopted by other conurbations during the early post-war period. They represented a response to the social and economic conditions of the time; in particular, acute pressures on land for peripheral development. If accommodated, such pressure led to the progressive suburbanisation of the countryside or unplanned sprawl which took good farmland and spoilt the appearance of the landscape. These problems were most in evidence on the fringes of the largest cities, especially London, and thus the rationale for Green Belts was clearest in the context of the problems facing the large city. Similar urban pressures arose on the peripheries of the industrial cities in the North of England and Scotland but for other reasons - large-scale greenfield development was needed for rehousing programmes consequent upon the removal of sub-standard and slum housing and poor urban environments.

None of these circumstances automatically dictated that Green Belts would follow - the formation (or non-formation) of Green Belts in different places at different times may have been coupled with that of the lobbying power of the Council for the Protection of Rural England (of which Abercrombie was an influential member).

Green Belts around large cities also arose from a strong anti-urban tradition long associated with the idea that society should improve housing and environmental standards. This idea reflects approaches to urban planning taken in the post-war period and was strongly influenced by the Barlow Commission, 1940, which recommended the urgent need for dispersal from London. Green Belt policy was therefore complementary to other urban policies devised to meet the changing needs of the population living in the conurbations, as Abercrombie demonstrated so eloquently in the Greater London Plan of 1944. Green Belts were an inevitable corollary of the need to deal with future urban growth by dispersal to planned new communities rather than by additions to the built-up edge, an approach strongly advocated by the Town and Country Planning Association in a paper called 'Dispersal: A Call for Action'.[3] Green Belt policy was seen, in principle at least, as an instrument for urban (containment) policy. Green Belts are still regarded by government as essentially an urban policy 'for shaping the expansion of a city on a regional scale'.[4]

It is important to distinguish the early ideas for Green Belts around large cities from the later and less consistent approach towards the establishment of Green Belts around smaller urban areas. Smaller Green Belts were proposed and implemented 'informally' during the late 1950s and 1960s, following the encouragement given in Circular 42/55 to local authorities outside London. But formal approval was very slow; many cities either never received it or had to wait until Green Belts were sanctioned in the development plans of the 1980s.

Why some smaller cities adopted Green Belt policies while others did not appears to be an under-researched question. Possibly it was due to a lack of clarity in government advice - 42/55 does not say what size of urban area merits a Green Belt. Small towns where growth pressures were not seen to be strong, such as Swindon, would not need them. Non-designation was partly a matter of accident - as in the Norwich case where an 'informal' Green Belt restriction was never for any obvious reason translated into a formal proposal - and was partly to do with other countryside and dispersal policies being seen to achieve the desired constraints on sprawl (Leicestershire and Cleveland are examples). The history of land ownership and political control in different regions may also have influenced local decisions.

In sum, Green Belt policies evolved mainly from pre-war and early post-war conditions and were applied with most vigour to the largest cities. It has been assumed that containment of an urban area to a particular size is desirable. No reasons have been advanced why the peripheral expansion of the larger cities/conurbations was undesirable when peripheral growth is an accepted feature of smaller towns, cities and even villages.

The main historical circumstances were:

- acute housing pressures within the largest cities;

- local authority programmes for public overspill on their peripheries;

- an upsurge in private house building especially during the early 1950s;

- ribbon development as a significant problem in the countryside;

- loss of farmland which enjoyed special protection at the time;

- firm belief in urban dispersal as a basis for urban policy;

- selective purchases of land for recreation; and

- the existence following the 1947 Town and Country Planning Act of planning controls which did not cover open land uses.

2

Green Belts in Reality

The expectations attached to Green Belts have not in our opinion been matched by reality. Although the expected outcomes of Green Belt policy are difficult to isolate from other factors, we find established policy faulty in a number of ways.

RESTRICTIONS ON ECONOMIC DEVELOPMENT

Fault One: Green Belts have restricted economic development in places and regions which need development.

The Green Belt is essentially a tool of physical planning policy unrelated to economic strategy. Blanket restraints on development, subject to certain exceptions, are applied by the Department of Environment and the local authorities in all Green Belts irrespective of their location, regional development needs or the interests of industrialists. There is thus a contradiction between Green Belt policy and government regional policy. There is no special presumption that industrial development is more acceptable in the northern Green Belts just because these are located in Assisted Areas nor that urban growth should be more strongly resisted in southern Green Belts because they are located in the prosperous South East.

The tendency of Green Belts to stifle or deflect industrial demand suggests they could have been used as a tool for national and regional policy in the same way that Industrial Development Controls (IDCs) were in the heyday of regional policy. The growth of new industry and commerce has been severely restricted by Green Belt policy (mainly to prevent the need for further housing in accordance with Circular 42/55). Fothergill's analysis of the London MGB refers to a probable loss of 14-23,000 manufacturing jobs in the MGB between 1974 and 1981 and potentially 100,000 over the life of the MGB.[5] Some new mobile investment could move elsewhere in the outer South East or to other parts of the UK although the small and medium-sized companies unable to move may be lost to the national economy if they cannot grow.

Industrialists have therefore grown to view Green Belts as a negative and restrictive force, both in those regions crying out for more development and in those where the economy is already 'overheated'. In regions suffering economic problems, exceptions have had to be made for major sites such as Kodak (Nottingham Green Belt), Nissan (Tyne and Wear Green Belt) and the new technology developments close to the M6/M42 interchange located in the confirmed West Midlands Green Belt. In such cases the government has argued that the advantage of new jobs outweighs the environmental argument for keeping the Green Belt free of built development. In the South East, restrictions on industrial and commercial development caused by the Green Belt are blamed for raising the economic costs of building sites around London, taking into account house-price inflation and labour shortages.[6] Opportunities for industrial development on damaged or derelict land within the Green Belt are missed even though places like the Thames Corridor are in urgent need of economic regeneration.

Government transport policy is equally unresponsive to regional economic conditions. Indeed, the location of transport infrastructure, especially the building of new and extended motorways, has been treated as an exceptional class of development which overrides Green Belt policy. In the West Midlands, before the region received Intermediate Area status, approval was granted for the new terminal at Birmingham Airport, the M40 and M42; more recently, consideration was given to the building of the northern orbital M6 and western M5 routes, and all projects affecting the Green Belt. In the South East, the M25 runs for its entire length through the London Metropolitan Green Belt. Such projects do much to alter the balance of regional economic advantage and disadvantage in the UK and also have enormous cumulative impact on the pressures for urban development within and beyond the Green Belt. As David White puts it, 'Green Belts have a habit of inventing roles for themselves. The metropolitan Green Belt, for example, has kept land open for the building of the M25, London's outer orbital motorway. The planners now say this is one of the benefits of Green Belt!'[7]

The Green Belt is a rigid national planning policy which is rarely modified to suit regional or local economic needs and is more often breached to allow infrastructure provision seen to be in the national interest. Sadly, these breaches are not a sign of government flexibility. They weaken the currently defined physical planning purposes of the Green Belt. Green Belts are not intended to be flexible. The legislation does not recognise that the Green Belt should be a flexible tool which may need to be modified to achieve regional objectives for urban development. If it did, this would imply that the Green Belt is not an end in itself but a means to control and steer certain forms of growth towards a desired pattern of regional economic and settlement change.

STRATEGIC PLANNING

Fault Two: Green Belts have been a weak instrument of regional strategic planning.

Green Belts should have been a central element of regional planning policy. The vision of purpose behind Abercrombie's 1944 Greater London Plan has not been sustained through the history of Green Belt policy development. Circular 42/55 made no reference to any regional role for the Green Belt. Instead, the Green Belt has been a strong negative power unrelated to the physical planning policies and machinery needed for managing decentralisation from cities.

The strategic planning objectives of the 1940s which have persisted for nearly half a century involved two simple, broad-brush spatial-planning objectives: protection of Green Belt and provision of planned growth beyond. However, Green Belts have been treated in effect, if not in intent, as a policy on their own. This has been due in part to the history of the legislation and in part to the way the boundaries have been extended in Sketch Map Green Belts. The London MGB - as David Lock points out in a recent paper - grew from a depth of about five miles in the Abercrombie Plan for Greater London, to seven to ten miles in the early 1950s, and to 20 miles in the late 1950s leading the government to accept 12-15 miles as a reasonable extent.[8]

Historical animosity over the scales and location of future urban growth has characterised relations between county and city authorities; local government reform in 1974 helped to sustain the counties' support for Green Belts while doing little to assist the integration of Green Belt with other policies at a urban-regional level.

Government legislation on Green Belts emerged without the policy co-ordination needed to achieve urban-regional planning objectives. The process whereby local authorities gained approval for the designation of Green Belts was never timed to coincide with the designation of New Towns or the selection of Expanded Towns schemes beyond the Green Belt. For example, the London MGB came on the scene well before the New Towns (1946) Act. In central Scotland, Cumbernauld was not designated a New Town until 1955, well after approval of the Clydeside Green Belt. After the 1955 Circular the submission and approval of Green Belts around the country was variable: in several regions the New Towns programme did not become really effective until the mid-1960s; in others Green Belts were not introduced until after a period of overspill policy.

The overspill programmes failed to match the scale of the city housing problems of the time and this encouraged short-term abandonment of the Green Belt: for example in the West Midlands the Green Belt was abandoned at Chelmsley Wood (1964) and Moundsley (1968) following decisions on 'appeal'. In the West Midlands:

> the end result, therefore, was in theory a strategy of containment but increasingly in practice a pragmatic combination of limited (belated) overspill into new and expanded towns, plus, on grounds of expediency, as well as for social and economic reasons, some substantial development 'in selected peripheral locations'.[9]

David Lock has suggested that the Green Belt worked well while there was a decentralisation policy intact.[10] But this is a rosy view of the past. The scale and number of schemes was totally inadequate for handling the housing pressures of the times. Those programmes which were implemented helped to some extent in meeting urban housing needs - most notably in Clydeside and Merseyside[11] - but around London and Birmingham the bulk of housing provision took place in locally designated 'growth' areas and smaller towns and villages both within and outside the Green Belts. The planned schemes played a marginal role in meeting urban housing requirements and there was never a time when they were able to provide regions with sufficient development land - as Lock suggests was the case around London during the 1950s, even if agreement can be reached on what represents an adequate supply of housing land at the regional scale.

THE COUNTRYSIDE BEYOND

Fault Three: Green Belts have forced too much growth on towns and villages beyond the Green Belts.

In the case of London and the West Midlands, Green Belt policy may be seen as successful in diverting growth to settlements beyond, thus contributing to a form of incremental urbanisation of the countryside. This is an argument increasingly advanced by some Conservative politicians and planners in areas undergoing rapid physical change e.g. Central Berkshire.[12] Development pressures have risen beyond the Green Belts surrounding provincial cities such as Nottingham or Bristol as land within Green Belt village envelopes runs out. Similar problems are evident on a different scale in Clydeside, Merseyside and Manchester.

Development beyond the Green Belt cannot really be viewed as a deliberate result of Green Belt policy since no reference was ever made in the legislation to their city-regional role. Green Belts have not been able to shape the spatial pattern of urban development in the countryside beyond. Nor was the siting of New Towns directly affected by Green Belt policy. That they have exerted an influence over the aggregate level of decentralised urban growth is however acknowledged implicitly by the emphasis now given to urban regeneration in Circular 14/84. In Scotland, the potential regional impact of Green Belts was recognised in Circular 40/60 and attempts were made to apply a similarly restrictive countryside policy beyond the outer boundaries of the Green Belt.

One difficulty in evaluating the role of Green Belts in managing decentralisation is that the Green Belts and areas beyond are often treated as two distinct categories of development change. In practice, there are many regional and local variations in patterns of development pressure and provision both within and outside Green Belts. There may be no direct relationship between the existence and extent of Green Belts and the degree of permanence represented by the policy. From the evidence available to us, it does not seem that all Green Belts have operated as a 'blanket restraint policy' in the manner assumed by the government and housebuilders. Similarly, it is oversimplistic to see all areas beyond the present Green Belts as being swamped by development pressures, especially in the North of England.

Whatever interpretation is taken of the effectiveness or otherwise of such policy in redirecting growth, neither the Green Belt nor the areas beyond are being planned to best advantage. There is, for example, an imbalance in policies for housing and employment. Employment is strongly controlled within the Green Belt but less so beyond; limited housing is allowed in Green Belts and much more is allowed outside. Hence there are social problems of housing need and provision which are not being addressed within the present boundaries and there are dual problems of 'over-heating' in some 'growth locations' as well as the under-provision of sites for low-cost housing in rural areas beyond the Green Belts. The view that Green Belts cannot be made permanent without provision for growth being made outside their boundaries serves to accentuate these imbalances in market demands and provision.

OPEN LAND AND RECREATION

Fault Four: Green Belts have done little to improve the appearance of open land or to promote the provision of recreation.

Improvement of their appearance was never a stated objective of the English Green Belt policy, although Circular 42/55 advises local authorities to pay special attention to visual amenity when considering proposals for development which will be in the Green Belt or conspicuous from it. Planning Policy Guidance Note 2 - Green Belts - is similarly somewhat ambivalent: it reaffirms the government view that 'the quality of the landscape is not a material factor in their designation or in their continued protection' (para 6) but accepts that the visual amenity of the Green Belt should be a consideration in determining proposals even if these do not prejudice the main purpose of the Green Belt (para 14). In Scotland, Circular 24/85 refers to 'maintaining the landscape setting of towns'.[13]

Central government has always subscribed to the negative view of Green Belts. It matters less what they look like than where they are. While these perceptions reinforce the primary containment role they fail to take account of the growing importance society attaches to environmental protection. Environmental enhancement has not been made an explicit objective of Green Belt policy, which is inconsistent with the government view that an attractive environment is important to the business world.[14]

In England, recreation provision has always been a secondary objective of Green Belt policy. In Scotland, a different approach is noticeable: one of the primary purposes is to provide countryside for recreation. The relationship between Green Belts policy and provision of recreation and public open space has been at best an indirect one. Some of the Countryside Commission management experiments took place in Green Belt areas. One limiting factor has been the prohibition on recreation buildings, with the exception of sports facilities. Another constraint on wider public provision is that most of the land in Green Belts is in private ownership and private owners have seen little value from investment in recreation, except possibly when linked to farm-based tourism. There is little public money for recreation provision and what *has* taken place has been opportunistic, with the result that sites are not always well located for maximum public use.[15] Surveys by the Countryside Commission have shown that half the visitors to such recreation sites live locally, i.e. within the Green Belt, nearly 75 per cent live within six miles but only 5 per cent come from the inner cities.[16] The problem of access is most acute around London where travel times and distances from the inner city to the Green Belt are greater than for other cities and where public transport services have become less frequent and more costly and do not reach the urban edge. As Polly Toynbee put it:

> where the underground lines once reached out to the countryside, with posters advertising day trips to green and grassy Hendon or Edgware, now the concrete has out stripped the tubes.[17]

RELATED POLICIES

Fault Five: Other policies have been as important as Green Belts in controlling urban development in the countryside.

The strength of present Green Belt policy appears to be its certainty and simplicity, particularly in areas under development pressure. But this view, commonly expressed by planning officers, does not altogether stand scrutiny. The classic studies carried out by Gregory and others[15] attempted to answer the question 'what if permissions had been granted rather than refused in Green Belts?' But they did not seek to analyse the importance of other non-Green Belt policies which apply in all countryside areas, or to compare the pattern of applications on Green Belt land with those in other rural areas.

General structure plan policies for rural development in the countryside seem remarkably similar to those policies which are supposed to apply to Green Belts. Perhaps this is more obvious where the range of 'permitted developments' in the Green Belt has become more liberal - but the differences between policies seem marginal to us. Rural settlement policies especially may play as important a part as Green Belt policy in restricting urban development and shaping urban areas.

Green Belt restrictions often complement or enhance rural settlement policies which to some extent place restrictions on development. Research in Warwickshire[19] compared adjacent designated Green Belt and undesignated countryside areas and suggested that there is little significant difference between permissions granted. In each case some 25 to 28 per cent of dwellings had been permitted. Settlements both inside and outside the Green Belt were affected by other settlement and countryside policies; for example, a 'key' settlement within the designated area had 41 dwellings allowed on appeal and only one refused, whereas 'other' settlements had no dwellings allowed on appeal and 135 refused. Hence, although development was resisted, the operation of another policy, settlement policy, was as important as Green Belt policy in controlling the scale and form of urban incursion. A separate analysis of the 'justification for permissions' in the designated and undesignated areas suggested some variations, however. In the Green Belt over 35 per cent were speculative or based on planning gain, compared with only 23 per cent outside the Green Belt. Local need was in fact the strongest reason for permitting development in the general countryside areas - 27 per cent, and was similar in the Green Belt areas at 29 per cent. Pre-existing policy commitments also accounted for a considerable number of permissions in the Green Belt, over 19 per cent. These were virtually non-existent in the general countryside areas. Overall the study concluded that greater pressure existed for development in the Green Belt than

outside it; but the designation did not deter applications sufficiently to reduce these below the total for the undesignated area.

We received evidence to argue that development change around cities
which have no Green Belt policy could be just as effectively controlled
through a combination of strategic and local planning policies, including
settlement policy, to channel development pressures, protect the countryside and provide for informal countryside recreation needs. In these examples, certainty against sprawl into the countryside was guaranteed if
developments were refused by the local authorities and their decisions were
clearly supported by central government. The existence of an up-to-date,
clearly understood and statutorily approved strategic policy was crucial. Thus
the Norfolk Structure Plan, approved in 1982, includes the following policy:
'any extensions to the built-up area of Norwich will ensure the maintenance
of a hard edge providing a clear boundary between town and country'. The
Leicestershire Structure Plan includes a 'green wedge' policy which provides
a rather more positive policy than many Green Belts. In Scotland the establishment of Green Belts was proposed in the relevant structure plans following local government reorganisation in 1975. Tayside Regional Council
proposed the abandonment of the Dundee Green Belt. Among other argu-
ments, the council maintained at the Examination in Public that the objectives of controlling urban sprawl, preventing the coalescence of built-up
areas and the protection and enhancement of the City's landscape setting
could be better achieved through other measures, including Countryside Policy; this was accepted by the Secretary of State in his decision letter of 6 April
1989 approving the Tayside Structure Plan.

3

Perceptions of Green Belts Today - Change or Continuity?

The consistency and persistence of a favourable image of Green Belts is notable, although the pioneering role attributed to them is no longer advocated.[20] Popularity may be due to the all-purpose attraction of the concept.

> It sounds as though Green Belts are all things to all men. That makes them seem an elusive, even devious device. But in fact it is surely a critical element of their attraction, and the key to understanding the longevity and popularity of the concept.[21]

Yet the public support for the Green Belts does not square easily with the catalogue of faults listed above. David Lock expresses a more critical view:

> I record my appreciation of the popularity of Green Belt as a planning concept, and my awareness that it is a policy that has been most willfully and cynically distorted, misrepresented, and abused for political purposes. It has been used, in my opinion, to manipulate people's feelings about towns, the countryside, and the tension that exists between them.[22]

There are still few who would publicly challenge the overall principle of Green Belts although there are differences in perceptions amongst the various bodies and interest groups which the central state has to mediate between. Local government also mediates but holds its own perceptions as well; part of the central-local tensions that have developed with the concept. To what extent do different groups perceive there to be faults with current policy?

CENTRAL GOVERNMENT

In England Green Belts are essentially seen as a tool for protecting the countryside. The faults in current policy go unacknowledged; indeed the reverse seems the case, with Mr Ridley currently proclaiming the successes of Green Belts. The new government publication on Green Belts refers to 'the success of Green Belt policy and the pleasure that these wide open spaces around our great cities afford to millions of people'.[23] We detect a rather more critical approach in Scotland and a greater awareness of the need to review the limitations of green belt policy as operating over the 25 years since 1960.

> Green Belts have become under increasing pressure: the countryside beyond Green Belts is now more accessible for residence, employment and leisure; and the types of development required or proposed are more varied than new houses with which Circular 40/1960 was mainly concerned ... new non-traditional activities are making an important contribution to the rural economy, and there is a need to encourage new economic activities.[24]

Following the 1979 change of government it seemed that Green Belt policy could be opened up for serious review. The existence of Green Belts did not seem to square with a greater emphasis on facilitative modes of planning and an ideology of quick land release. However, any potential threat to the sanctity of the concept was clarified in Circular 22/80 which argued that:

> the Government continues to attach great importance to the use of Green Belts to contain the sprawl of built-up areas and to safeguard the neighbouring countryside from encroachment and there must continue to be a general presumption against any inappropriate development within them.[25]

The draft circulars issued in 1983 encouraged the popular view that Green Belts might be sacrificed; these were withdrawn after political protest and the House of Commons Environment Committee reviewed revised draft circulars.[26]

Circular 14/84 reaffirmed the original terms of the Green Belt and added a new role of promoting urban regeneration. Green Belts are now seen to have an additional purpose - the redirection of investment pressures inwards rather than outwards. This change in policy may reflect some concern about the pressure on areas beyond Green Belts but we think it is more an acknowledgement of the point made by local authorities in the West Midlands and North of England, notably Manchester, that outward pressures have fallen off and regeneration should be supported. It is also a logical consequence of the abandonment of the planned programmes for decentralisation and fits in with the government's recent commitment to urban revitalisation.

There is little evidence that the effect of Circular 14/84 has been to harden-up Green Belt controls as interpreted through the development plan system, although there appears to have been a more consistent refusal of major proposals around London in the last few years e.g. the new settlement at Tillingham Hall and the rejection of proposed out-of-town shopping and leisure centres at the 'Golden Triangle' site near the M1/M25 junction, Waterdale Park, Bricket Wood and at Hewitts Park, Orpington.[27]

One important arena for examining central government's perception of Green Belt now lies within the development plan system. The concept was enshrined in the new Town and Country Planning Acts of 1968-72 with incorporation of Green Belts into formal Structure Plan statements and the locally negotiated process for determining their boundaries through Local Plans (Green Belt Subject Plans). An aspect of the latest government advice affects the extent of Green Belt boundaries. In several regions, the West Midlands being a classic case, the detailed boundaries of Green Belt have never been formally approved by government - instead 'interim' Green Belts were approved under the old development plans. There is a strong presumption in 14/84 that these 'interim' boundaries may now be rolled back to allow for future development needs, as defined in Local Plans; this could lead to a random and piecemeal pattern of urban development. Additional uncertainty is prompted by the government's proposed reform of development plans insofar as the new County Statements appear to have no statutory force.[28]

Another arena is privatisation; in particular, government attitudes to the disposal of publicly owned land especially where this is located in Green Belt. Circular 12/87 - 'Redundant Hospital Sites in the Green Belt' - issued guidelines and the future use of redundant hospital sites is referred to in PPG2. The Shenley and Napsbury sites in Hertfordshire illustrate the renegotiation of some Green Belt land which is now taking place. The disposal of British Aerospace land within the Green Belt raises potentially similar issues.

Some recognition of changes in the rural economy is noticeable in the government's response to redundant farm buildings (para 16, PPG2) which tells local authorities not to refuse permission for re-use unless there are 'specific and convincing reasons which cannot be overcome by attaching conditions to the planning permission'. Conversion to houses or new business uses will help new enterprise, especially small business.

LOCAL AUTHORITIES

The West Midlands Forum of County Councils sums up the approach of many local authorities towards Green Belts:

> traditionally the Green Belt has been seen by planning authorities within the conurbations as a constraint to development whilst authorities in the Green Belt and those beyond its outer edge have seen it as a vital protection against the powerful forces of urban development.[29]

Shire Counties have been well aware of the incursions taking place in their areas. The extent of physical change which has been accommodated in Green Belts is well illustrated from analysis of actual planning approvals and refusals during the years 1979-83 in the West Midlands Green Belt.[30] Some local authorities seek to tighten policy by expanding the criteria used in the Green Belt Circulars (often resulting in the Secretary of State reducing draft designations); others take the view that Green Belts are unnecessary and that other countryside and restraint policies have served just as well, although this is difficult to demonstrate. Exceptions to the Green Belt have been advocated by local authorities from time to time, usually to remove individual settlements or land parcels on the inner or outer fringes deemed to be unsuitable for designation. The blanket nature of DoE approaches to Green Belt policy have been a source of irritation where local authorities see a good case for modifying the interpretation of national policy to meet regional or local needs. We were given several examples:

Cheshire sought to introduce greater flexibility in the Structure Plan review to allow existing firms to expand or redevelop, minor small-scale development for employment and starter firms, and tourist facilities in the Green Belt. Chester City Council sought to remove 200 acres of designated Green

Belt to permit a wide range of industrial and residential uses, a policy which has recently been rejected following a public local inquiry.[31]

Nottinghamshire County Council at the time of its Structure Plan Examination in Public also sought to encourage new employment development in areas where a need was likely to arise, including land within the Green Belt, but the Secretary of State has conceded that such a policy would be contrary to the objectives and function of the Green Belt. Kent has unsuccessfully attempted, through the development plan system, to renegotiate the Green Belt as a tool for achieving urban development in the Dartford area of the Eastern Thames Corridor. The District Plan for Dartford sought to remove 800 hectares (2,000 acres) of largely damaged and disused Green Belt land from designation (of which 230 hectares was for business use and housing with commercial leisure and recreation uses on the remainder). CPRE challenged this proposal on the basis that it would act as a precedent against the green belt concept. The London Planning Advisory Committee (LPAC) also saw a threat to inner urban regeneration policy.[32] The government has thrown out the proposals.

Metropolitan Counties became increasingly involved before abolition with overcoming problems of land management and lack of recreation provision in their areas and other local authorities have taken up these themes.[33] The appearance of the countryside in Green Belt, land management issues and public control was particularly pertinent in Scotland. We noted the role of the Edinburgh Green Belt agreement[34] and the Clyde Calders project[35] where we detected that the perception of open land policy and Green Belt policy in general was rather was different from England.

Local authorities may be aware of the failings of strategic planning and the social divisiveness of Green Belt policy but their willingness and ability to modify Green Belt policy is very limited. Our impression is that tight national interpretation of Green Belts in England inhibits any development of a regional role for Green Belts despite the authorities' interest in negotiating changes in policy through the Structure Plan process.

DEVELOPERS

Developers have increasingly emphasised that Green Belts do nothing of themselves to protect the quality of the landscape.

A distinction is sometime drawn between the positive and negative aspects of the Green Belt. While many parts of the established Green Belts are worth saving, there is still much 'brown belt' which would be better redeveloped for retail, leisure and business parks, with agreements to green over other derelict land. 'Green Belts have come to enjoy a political sanctity similar to that of national parks' ... 'Well designed industrial, retail or residential developments in parkland settings must surely outrank in public good an agri-business of concrete silos and ugly sheds set in a landscape denuded of hedges and trees.'[36]

Although developers are viewed by the conservation lobby as willing to sacrifice the Green Belt in the interests of housebuilding and, to a lesser extent, commercial and leisure-facility expansion, they claim that the concept provides a degree of certainty and security. Hence limited planning regulation is seen as acceptable together with a minimum of conservation. John Newman, London and Edinburgh Trust PLC has commented:

> May I state unequivocally that in both a corporate and personal sense, I am a committed supporter of the Green Belt. My company ... recognises that attention to landscaping and environment surrounding the building will produce both personal satisfaction and commercial dividends. We are not in the business of vandalising attractive tracts of land but seek to satisfy ascertainable public demands for buildings whether they be retail, commercial or residential by creating attractive developments which pay proper respect to their surroundings.[37]

The Green Belt is not seen as sacrosanct. Parcels of it, particularly on the inner fringe, are viewed as vulnerable, often on grounds of degradation, and a whole series of challenges to the concept have occurred on these sites, especially in the South-East. Some developers are unhappy in England about the relationship between land-release policies and the extent of restrictive countryside designations, especially the Green Belt.[38] In London and the South East they have been ahead of local planning authorities in drawing attention to the extension of the MGB in addition to the many existing kinds of countryside restraint and conservation policy and the limitationns these pose upon strategic planning for the location of future urban growth. Some volume house builders have sought to promote new country towns beyond the Green Belt, the cost in their eyes of preserving the concept intact. In contrast, we heard evidence from the West Midlands that established large corporations (superstores, sand and gravel extraction, speculative industrial projects) were confidently pursuing planning approval despite the hostile attitudes of the Green Belt lobby.

ENVIRONMENTAL GROUPS

There are powerful and effective coalitions of interest groups supportive of Green Belt policy as a means of stopping development in the countryside. Many groups are involved at a local level, including the Country Landowners Association, National Farmers Union, MAFF, County Councillors, District Councillors, Parish Councillors, Local Authority Officers at various levels, ratepayers and residents associations, local amenity groups and local MPs.

The narrow perception of the issues is evident. They are mainly concerned with stopping development, although some groups wish to see a more positive provision for conservation and management of land within the Green Belt. We would have expected greater challenge on social grounds to proposals affecting Green Belt settlements, especially the lack of housing for locals, insofar as this could be seen as a tool for mitigating the risks of poorly designed suburban housing layouts and effecting a slowdown in the rate of physical change; we expected the urban-regeneration argument would be embraced more fully.

The CPRE sees Green Belts as the cornerstone of the defence of 'countryside' and the rural idyll. Their approach seems to be to conserve everything rather than risk destroying something that may be valued later.[39]

Even if Green Belt landscapes are damaged or derelict they are seen as preferable to urban intrusion - hence a blanket policy is favoured, which says little about the content of Green Belt and access to it. The CPRE is highly critical of proposals for new urban development which would reduce the existing extent of Green Belts. Smaller regional and local pressure groups tend to mimic the CPRE attitude, arguing that open space has inherent value in itself and should be conserved. Some, such as the London Green Belt Council, exist primarily to monitor planning applications within the MGB, and seek to defend the clearly defined goals of the concept.

The goal of countryside protection and enhancement underpins the perception of environmental interest groups. Management schemes and recreation planning may fulfil these goals as well as simple urban containment. The environmental issue is becoming diffused with other concerns about agricultural change. Voluntary action groups play a role within the Green Belt e.g. the Groundwork Trusts.

In sum, many of the faults of current Green Belt policy are ignored. The image of the Green Belt 'as a band of rustic tranquillity' appears to lead perceptions, and the policy remains essentially unaltered, namely:

- protection against urban growth - a key role as central government sees it;

- negotiation of boundaries and to a lesser extent permitted uses through the local planning process, as the local authorities see it;

- development on 'brown belt land,' but within existing Green Belts, as some developers see it;

- stopping urban development, conservation and management of open land as environmentalists see it.

Green belt policies evolved mainly from pre-war and early post-war conditions - there is still no perception of the need to review the policy or to modify it in a way which would make it more relevant to the policy issues of today, i.e. responding to the new geography of industry and population and the new political profile of the environment.

4

The Context for Green Belts in the Future

The circumstances which gave rise to Green Belts around our big cities have altered, yet perception of the need for Green Belts has remained obstinately persistent. The concept has become enshrined in planning thought and there is little evidence that, despite the massive changes which have affected Britain's spatial economy during the past forty years, anyone is willing to confront the question: are Green Belts an appropriate tool for dealing with today's problems? In our view they are not and we believe that the concept of Green Belts needs modifying in a way which will bring it up to date. To judge this requires some appraisal of the issues which challenge the present concept. This is bound to be selective but we consider there are six key issues which must be addressed.

1. OUTER METROPOLITAN GROWTH

The establishment of Green Belts as 'stoppers' against the physical spread of large cities was perhaps inevitable given historic patterns of urban growth. Policy was directed inwards towards the pressures seen to be emanating from the conurbations. Since the 1940s fundamental changes in the urban and regional system have taken place.

Growth at the edge of large cities has been followed by growth around the fringes of many smaller towns and villages in the more distant countryside. Social and geographical mobility, primarily the decentralisation of population beyond the Green Belt, the shift in employment opportunity and the relative failure of new towns to be self-contained have all contributed to these patterns although there are regional variations in the scale and kind of dispersed urban growth and in the nature of the consequent pressures on the countryside.[40]

These trends mean that the Green Belt as originally conceived - for stopping development pressures on the edge of the largest cities - has become an outdated concept for controlling pressures for urban growth which are felt across wide areas of lowland rural England, well beyond the boundaries of the confirmed Green Belts and well beyond the peripheries of the conurbations.[41] The danger of these trends is that they lead to a form of incremental urbanisation of the countryside characterised by the tacking of development on to every town and village in the South East. These risks are well understood by local authority planners and local politicians in outer metropolitan areas undergoing rapid physical change both in Scotland[42] and England.

2. THE REDUCTION OF FARMLAND

A future Green Belt of undisturbed agriculture providing an attractive setting for urban populations is now quite unrealistic. Less farmland will be required in the future and a complete reappraisal of countryside planning policies which seek to protect farmland against urban change is taking place. The scale of the future problem is noted in the Glasgow Green Belt, for instance, where farming, market gardening and agriculture are no longer as important as they used to be, meaning that large areas of Green Belt land may cease to have a productive purpose in the future.[43] Some land will be required for tourism, interpretation and nature conservation. Some may be used for forestry, informal recreation, sports facilities and various forms of built development, housing and local industry. Current English legislation, Circular 16/17 'Development Involving Agricultural Land' places emphasis on the need to facilitate economic activity that provides jobs but to continue protecting the countryside for its own sake rather than primarily for the productive value of the land. Current Green Belt policy appears to follow this advice only in respect of redundant farm buildings (PPG2 para 16).

3. RURAL HOUSING CRISIS

Green Belts were introduced at a time of acute housing shortages within the largest cities. Today such problems still exist in the cities and there are new problems of household formation in the growing communities outside the cities and a diminishing supply of affordable housing in the countryside.[44]

The consequences of high house- and land-price inflation are found throughout lowland England and parts of Wales and are by no means confined to Green Belts. Until alternative approaches are found some developers will continue to build expensive houses and the problem of buying land cheap enough to build low-cost housing will remain. Targeting of resources and greater flexibility in the release of sites is implied in the Department of Environment's more recent advice on low cost housing.[45] Local authorities are asked to release small sites where cheap accommodation is needed with rules to ensure housing stays local.[46] The Green Belts as presently conceived do not allow for any flexibility in the provision of new low-cost housing.

We would not hold the Green Belt entirely responsible for problems of access to housing, which has resulted from the national reduction in social housing (itself reflecting enhanced priority given to owner occupation and cutbacks in public expenditure). However these processes have impacted particularly on such groups as single persons, one-parent families and the elderly who already face limited housing and employment opportunities in the Green Belts as well as historically high house prices.

The defence of the conservation ethic by established resident groups, particularly in settlements enveloped within the Green Belt, highlights the social problems which still arise. The Green Belt is used by these groups, in combination with local authorities, as a form of symbolic defence against any form of change. But this view ignores the effects Green Belts have on the protection of rural communities and landscapes - for example, restricted access to the housing market, restrictions on local job opportunities, social bias, decline of services, recreation and land-management problems. Particular social problems do appear to occur where Green Belt controls over housing developments have been consistently strong, or have hardened over time, i.e. where considerable 'white envelopes' were left within the Green Belt (as part of a rural settlement policy) and land for expansion has run out. Keyworth in the Nottingham Green Belt is one such example: additional urban growth is possible by virtue of local services (and some local jobs), but this has been resisted by unrepresentative local protection groups, despite the advantages extra development could bring in helping meet local housing needs.

4. CHANGES IN THE RURAL ECONOMY

Structural and spatial changes in the economy - particularly the decline of cities and the urban-rural shift in employment and population - have been associated with new kinds of pressure for urban development in the open countryside, for residence, employment and leisure. These trends are occurring throughout the space economy and have had particular impact on the rural economy. This is now undergoing fundamental change, with new non-traditional activities, small businesses, home-working, and tourism all playing a role, assisted by the government's policies for rural enterprise.[47]

Green Belts cannot remain immune from the events occurring in the rural economy. Pressures from the events taking place within the agricultural industry present new challenges for established policy. Farmers need to find new uses for farmland and farm buildings but, in the absence of planning control, may be encouraged to fragment their land into several small-holdings leading to a scattered pattern of single dwellings. The establishment of 'Farm Parks' for well-landscaped industrial workshops and specialist agricultural production could provide a planned response to the pressure for new uses of farmland.[48]

5. REGIONAL PRESSURE FOR COUNTRYSIDE DEVELOPMENT

New kinds of property-market pressure are being felt in the countryside, both within the present Green Belts and beyond their boundaries. However, there is a link between the existence of these pressures and changing regional economic performance. We detect a much greater level of aggregate demand for housing and leisure growth in London and the South East than in other regions where pressure for new retailing is stronger.

In terms of housing, major schemes have been identified in London and the rest of the South East (ROSE) in or just beyond the Green Belt. Of these, two have already been granted planning permission (one on appeal) and both lie within the Green Belt (Brenthall Park, Harlow and Chafford Hundred, Essex). Of the others Stone Bassett, Oxford (beyond that city's Green Belt) and Foxley Wood, Hampshire seem likely to be rejected. Although only a handful of these are a direct challenge to the Green Belt concept, all the proposals relate indirectly to some aspect of its principles. The difficulty of gaining planning approval within the Green Belt, reinforced for new free-standing proposals since Tillingham Hall, has driven developers beyond. At the same time dissatisfaction with incremental planning of existing settlements has generated the notion of new villages and towns, private- rather than public-sector-led.[49]

Within the London Metropolitan Green Belt a number of large-scale proposals for integrated commercial/leisure developments have been identified. These included at the time of writing:

1. STOCKLEY PARK, HILLINGDON - 18-hole golf course with an amenity centre and business park. Includes participatory sports and equestrian centre.

2. GRESHAM PARK, OSTERLEY (Northern edge, near Heathrow Airport) - housing and retail scheme, with around 350 hectares dedicated to leisure and parkland uses.

3. THEALE (READING) - more than three-quarters of the 810 hectares proposed for water-based sports, golf country club and other passive recreation.

4. BROOKLANDS RACE COURSE - mixed business/retail/leisure with participatory sports.

5. IVER (M25/M4 near Heathrow Airport) - out-of-town retail and leisure scheme with British Rail link.

Others included: Lakeside Centre, Thurrock; Blue Water Park, Dartford; Leybourne Park, West Malling, Kent; Elmbridge Mall, Hook; Tanhouse Pits, Colnbrook; and Sundon Springs, Bedfordshire.[50] Other smaller schemes have been proposed, often in conjunction with infrastructure developments such as the M25. A typical example is a proposal to use farmland fragmented by a new link to the M1 near Watford for mixed leisure uses.

These proposals may have no special advantages which override national and local Green Belt policies, as is evident in the Secretary of State's recent refusal of planning permission for two major shopping and leisure complexes at Bricket Wood in Hertfordshire and Hewitts Farm, Chelsfield, Orpington (see Chapter 3).

6. LOCAL AND REGIONAL STYLES OF PLANNING

Local flexibility will always exist in Green Belt policy, modifications to which take two forms: those approved by statute through revisions of Local Plans (and their predecessors) and those that result from successful planning applications within designated areas, directly or by appeal. The first type has generally occurred as part of the normal process of plan revision in the light of changing social and economic needs and the impact of other planning policies.

Although official Green Belt policy remains unresponsive to regional and sub-regional variations in economy or development pressure, we detect a growing challenge from local authorities to redress this situation and to bring about a more realistic regionally based approach to policy formulation. This pattern may develop further in the future, despite government reluctance to clarify 'permitted uses' or 'other uses appropriate to a rural area' - an issue raised by the House of Commons Environment Committee.[51] In practice, variations have been negotiated between local authorities and central government in the context of Structure Plan approvals and reviews. For example, the DoE's modifications to the South East Dorset Structure Plan, 1980, reflects the sub-regional role of tourism and allowed for non-intensive recreation, holiday chalets, caravans and tents; Derbyshire County Council acknowledged the expansion of small industrial firms, and new small industries in existing buildings, as well as public utilities, mineral working and waste disposal in the south Derbyshire Green Belt.[52]

There are changing interpretations of Green Belt policy between north and south. In the South East some incursions into Green Belt were negotiated in the early 1980s in the context of rising unemployment and recession, even in relatively prosperous areas. The economy is now growing and the case for land release has receded in general terms, though there are many localities in desperate need of regeneration, both in new jobs and housing. The main problem today is the imbalance between areas of growth and decline within the South East. In the Midlands incursions into the Green Belt may have reflected a somewhat desperate response to the recession or anxiety that the new policies for diverting growth into the conurbation would be insufficient to restore jobs. Today there is recognition of an improving economic base and the need to review Green Belt policy in a much wider spatial context than that which is provided by the old Metropolitan County boundaries.[53]

POLITICAL SALIENCE OF GREEN BELTS

The high political profile and strong public favour enjoyed by Green Belts are based partly on idealised images of rural life and landscape. Green Belts are seen as defences for these threatened values, and this has come to be regarded as their primary purpose. In fact, protection of the countryside in this way is seen as an end in itself, regardless of any contrary intention stated in government legislation.

Defence of this type has remained strong within the Green Belts - note the example of Tillingham Hall - but the pressures for growth outside are being resisted in a similar way. The protection of countryside, whether it is official Green Belt or not, has become a noticeable feature of political conflict over land release. In part there is no difference in the public mind between Green Belt and green-field sites anywhere. There are no clear symbols or signs in the landscape to identify where designated Green Belts begin or end and it is therefore understandable that everyone sees their local countryside as 'green belt'. As Geoffrey Collins, puts it:

> many people who live adjoining open green areas think that they adjoin or are in the Green Belt when they are not. Others consider that if they are in the Green Belt then that land is a recreation area for them to use quite regardless of its ownership by private individuals.[54]

What should we make of these widespread environmental values? Susan Clifford has pointed out that landscape features, whatever their 'official' designation and however unattractive they may be to the outsider, may assume a special value for local communities and require a recognition by policy makers.[55]

These factors help to explain the geographical spread of 'NIMBYism' and the growing political conflict over land beyond, as opposed to within, the Green Belt. 'The controversy is not about the Green Belt, but about green fields beyond. Not about whether some should disappear but how many, where and at what rate'.[56] There are those who insist that the existing and designated Green Belts should remain sacrosanct and those who would argue that present boundaries are irrelevant for dealing with the wider geographical spread of urban pressures.

5

Finding New Roles for Green Belts

The original case for Green Belts was based upon the understanding that the pressing urban problems of the time were associated with the growth of conurbations. Urban policy was unidirectional - outward dispersal was desirable. Green Belts became a necessary corollary. Today urban pressures have a regional and inter-regional dimension. Growth takes place across wide tracts of rural and lowland England, well beyond the big cities. Urban policy has changed - the inner city has been discovered. 'The Government now places much more emphasis on the regeneration and redevelopment of the older urban areas than on decentralisation'.[57] It is because of this changing geographical and policy context that we need to rethink the rationale for Green Belts.

Dispersal from large cities can no longer be the key concept behind such areas. There is a more complex process at work in the urban regions which involves the redistribution of population and employment, both within the fringe and to/from smaller free-standing towns. In our view a management strategy is required for dealing with the new development demands, whether for housing, retail or industrial development which arise from inter-regional shifts in household and employment relocation and commuting.

The purpose of Green Belts is still geared towards the separation of major conurbations from surrounding settlements. Hence the outward spread of small cities and towns is totally neglected. This raises a fundamental and under-researched issue, namely: is there a particular size beyond which a city ought not to grow, and why is peripheral expansion of the larger cities/conurbations thought undesirable when it is an accepted feature of smaller town and cities, and even villages?

ISSUES FOR FUTURE POLICY

Re-directing the Green Belt concept towards the management of outer urban change

Urban containment raises many fundamental problems when we come to evaluate the continuing relevance of Green Belts. The House of Commons Environment Committee's report on Green Belts and Housing Land, published in 1984, acknowledges the problem:

> the third objective of containing urban sprawl is the most difficult. At what point must further expansion be constrained? Most demand for Green Belts in the future is likely to come from modern expanding towns, such as those along the M4 corridor. At what point in their expansion should growth be stopped is therefore crucial to future Green Belt policy. When does urban growth become urban sprawl?[58]

The Environment Committee did not answer their own question except to profer the solution that development on peripheral sites may be judged to make inefficient use of land when there is still room for development within the urban area. However, if 'virtually all urban areas have some room for development' as they suggest, why should not all areas justify Green Belts? The answer may be that not all urban authorities have policies for urban regeneration; only where these exist will there be an additional case for Green Belts. This reinforces the weaknesses of present Green Belt policy - namely that it is mainly directed toward the largest cities.

Two aspects of sprawl were important to the early Green Belt idea: fear of ribbon development and loss of farmland due to urban development. Ribbon growth was largely associated with pre-planning days - most local authorities can in our view avoid it by using existing planning powers without recourse to Green Belt policy. The agricultural value of farmland was at stake in the 1940s; today the conservation of the countryside for its own sake is the issue. Urban development might rapidly remove the gaps between settlements and destroy such countryside if the statutory protection afforded by a Green Belt or a similar policy was removed.

The conservation role today is at least as important as the old containment function, a point recognised by the Countryside commission in 'Planning for a Green Countryside' (1988). But Green Belts cannot fulfil this role at present. Firstly, they cover only a small percentage of countryside - the quality of which may be no higher than that around smaller towns and cities outside the presently designated Green Belts. Second, Green Belt is a tool of land-use planning but some of the most important changes in the country-side do not require planning approval.

Green Belts as a framework for city-regional planning

Urban growth may become sprawl when there is no effective public planning system for regulating the location, scale and siting of future growth or redirecting it to alternative locations. In a sense the case for Green Belts must be made within the context of an effective strategic framework which takes into account housing demands and the spatial pattern of settlements over a wide geographical area.

Green Belts were never intended to be negative 'stoppers' to urban growth, as affirmed by the Environment Committee:

> We consider Green Belts have a broad and positive planning role: that of open spaces whose presumption against development can better shape urban areas, particularly on a regional scale.[59]

But which urban areas? The largest cities where growth has slowed down or the many smaller places where growth is booming? In our view the future of Green Belts must be seen against the background of outer metropolitan variations in housing demand and supply because the large cities play a diminished role in generating housing needs and pressures at a regional scale. We need a new regional planning role for Green Belts now that the policy of planned dispersal has been dropped.

One approach is to seek a more active role for Green Belts in the context of urban regeneration. Particularly where there is serious urban decline, Green Belts could take on the job of directing pressure inwards, as Strathclyde's policy has demonstrated. Sixty per cent of private sector housing was on redeveloped sites in 1985 compared to 27 per cent in 1978.[60] The problem with applying this approach in all regions is that the Green Belt has had time to become a Janus-faced concept with potential effects both beyond the outer boundaries and within the inner ones. In England, and especially in the Midlands and the South, the expansion of housing and employment continues apace beyond the Green Belts and cutting across administrative boundaries. Should this matter or should it be taken as a measure of the success

of Green Belt policy? It certainly matters if decentralisation and urban regeneration are mutually exclusive policy goals, as implied by the government's latest statement on Green Belts. The problem is that government
lacks a clear vision of what to do about decentralisation, which doesn't stop
simply because the policy goals have changed.

Relating Green Belt policy to regional problems

We would suggest that there may need to be different contexts for Green
Belt in the North and in the South. In the South, metropolitan expansion cuts
across traditional administrative boundaries and will force a redefinition of
the London region.[61]

The 'ring fence' approach to the growth of the South East has been con-
demned by the government but we should see solutions to the pressures on
land in the south within the context of a regional approach to public policy.
At present the MGB is used as a political weapon for diverting growth elsewhere within the South East. This passes the buck for handling growth from
one set of Shire Counties to another, and the counties outside the Green Belt
may be as unwilling to accept further growth as those within it. The Green
Belt should be shaping urban patterns within the extended London region.
It should be a flexible tool for resolving imbalances within the region - hold-
ing back the economic expansion in some areas while introducing more flexibility in the planning system elsewhere.

At the same time there is renewed interest in the North/South divide and
the need to respond to observed regional disparities. We see a connection
between Green Belts and the regional problem, which is essentially a problem of the industrial conurbations in the North. Because the Green Belt has
been approached solely as a tool for urban policy its potential for redirecting
resources at an inter-regional scale, in conjunction with other policy instru-
ments, has never seriously been considered. Would it be possible to restate
Green Belt policy in a way which would reflect the different metropolitan
and rural conditions applying in the South and yet complement the existing
urban regenerative function of Green Belts around northern cities?

Relating Green Belt policy to open land policy

Planning policy for the countryside was shaped by the influential Scott Report of 1942. Farming and forestry have been strongly protected and build-

ing in the countryside limited to larger settlements. Restrictions on the urban development of *open land* were virtually as strong as those imposed by Green Belt policy. Today, the realisation that agricultural production should be curbed rather than encouraged is producing a new policy agenda for open land - whether for new forests, recreation and tourism or alternative uses for redundant buildings. There are no longer special reasons why the character and quality of open land within Green Belts should not be kept on the sidelines from new thinking about the future of rural land.

SOME NEW APPROACHES

Green Belts are no longer 'at the crossroads' in quite the same way as in 1983/4 at the time of the House of Commons Environment Committee review. But although the government appears to have strengthened its determination to maintain Green Belts, the pro-development lobby continues to test the planning system, not only in Green Belt areas but in all greenfield sites with potential and some brownfield sites in designated areas as well. As the previous section suggested, Green Belt areas cannot be immune from the economic changes affecting the countryside as a whole. As an instrument for legitimating public concern about the environment the Green Belt *concept* still has currency but the Green Belt *policy* is hopelessly outdated.

Unfortunately, the scope for changing current green policy seems somewhat daunting. Some may think existing policies are adequate. Others, whilst acknowledging the need for change, still prefer the retention of these policies. We felt that discussion about the future of the Green Belts could not be separated from the wider debate within the professional organisations about the future of planning in general[62] and the perceived case for clearer national and regional guidelines.[63]

We are convinced of the need for a new direction for existing Green Belt policy. This needs to take account of three changes in circumstances since the early Green Belts were proposed:

- the altered geographical pattern of population and employment which embraces small as much as large settlements;

- the problem of the relative decline in the economic base of the big cities;

- the growing political salience of environmental issues.

We examined several options, none of which are mutually exclusive.

No change in present policy

With little flexibility to relax Green Belt status, now apparent from recent appeals, the development industry will look towards other countryside areas where development potential is available. If demands for free-standing settlements and other forms of urban development are satisfied there is a danger that in a few years the present Green Belts will simply become small islands of extreme protection, still fulfilling their apparent 'stopper' role for large centres but having little influence on the new forms of development consequent upon the urban-rural shift.

More selective use of present Green Belt policy

It has been suggested that the Metropolitan Green Belt should be reduced in size by half while additional Green Belts should be tacked on to other small towns.[64] We would then see an increase in the area of land unprotected by Green Belt and possibly many more new settlements developing, though with wedges of protection around all of them. However, we see this as a solution designed mainly to deal with the new dynamics of change in the South East. It does recognise the existence of urban-rural shift but in our view still risks continuation of the present overly negative view of the stopper role of Green Belts in regional planning. Nor does it deal with the growing need for improving landscape quality within the Belts or the problem of environmental opposition outside their boundaries.

Greening the Green Belt

We recognise the complexity of land-use change in the Green Belts, a subject which has been extensively researched in the case of London.[65] While many existing land uses will continue in the future, we believe in looking at new development and land-use possibilities within designated areas in order to improve the quality of environment in the countryside. We expect that in the future Green Belts will need to emphasise environmental values more strongly in a number of directions:

- extension of the principle of zoning in the countryside, with zoning and landscape plans to allocate and manage land for agriculture, forestry, leisure and small-scale urban developments;

- limited relaxations of current policy to allow reclamation of damaged and derelict sites; we recognise that landowners might let their land become derelict to get a higher value and we suggest a tight definition of the sort of derelict site to be included and restrictions on the time-period over which dereliction must have occurred before reclamation can take place;

- a pro-active approach toward recreation and open land improvement within Green Belts, i.e. on the lines of the Clyde Calders project in Scotland and the Countryside Commission's 'groundwork' exercises in England;

- extension of the present boundaries to provide for a variety of urban recreational needs and to protect the countryside: the greater use of green wedges is favoured, as in the West Midlands, but they should penetrate both within the conurbation and outwards between the settlements rapidly growing in the outer city. In addition we see the 'set-aside' idea as presenting the opportunity to review the nature of land uses within the Green Belt, although this review should not be confined to areas directly affected by set-aside.

Modification of Green Belt principles within a policy for general countryside change.

We considered raising the standing of Green Belt status beyond that of a narrowly defined land-use so as to incorporate a wider range of permitted uses than at present (some local authorities are already doing this). We were impressed by the Scottish approach which is aimed at the integration of policies for the Green Belt with those for the countryside in general. It was also interesting that the Green Belt idea had lost favour in Dundee in preference to a general countryside policy which was proving as effective on appeal. We did not find much difference in practical terms between the implementation of Green Belt and countryside policy in England. Indeed, countryside policies may be more restrictive in relation to housing or employment than Green Belt.

We also agreed with the Environment Committee's reference to the potential of Green Belts to shape regional patterns of urban growth. But the changing geography of urban growth strongly suggested that the present boundaries were irrelevant to this purpose. We were forced to question the traditional concept of a narrowly defined belt, with strongly protected countryside within and much more extensive urban growth in alternative locations outside. This was creating a false dualism in policy between some areas strongly conserved and others, perhaps more worthy of protection, being opened up for development, simply because they were not in the Green Belt. There were areas within Green Belts which could be developed without detriment to the landscape setting (the Dartford area of Kent being a good example) and areas outside the Green Belts where insensitive building could damage the environment (the undulating Wolds area of Leicestershire for instance). All countryside outside the conurbations is affected by the pressures of urban and rural change to a greater or lesser extent and there is no longer a special case for protecting countryside on the immediate edge of conurbations at the expense of other countryside further away from the big cities. Thus we saw the need for a policy which had a much greater geographical coverage than present Green Belt policy, an area which reflected the spatial reality of the spreading city.

Herein lay a dilemma: if the purpose of the Green Belt was to stop urban development, where would urban expansion go in an enlarged or altered Green Belt? Under the present policy Green Belts can only be kept permanent if sufficient land is found elsewhere. But this is because they restrict most forms of development. We argued that present policy was unduly negative and that a greater range of developments should be permitted in the countryside. The central issue was the current lack of a strategic framework for managing future scales, rates and forms of change in the countryside in the absence of a Green Belt. To resolve this required a greater integration between policies for conservation and economic development in *all* areas of the countryside. We saw the need both to abandon the restrictions of current Green Belts policy and to extend the concept to areas not now affected by Green Belts. This could only be done if strategic guidance was strengthened and upheld by central government. Sufficient land for economic development would need to be allocated within 'green' areas rather than outside them, as at present - an apparent paradox which could be resolved by modifying current Green Belt policy.

In our view a radical rethink of Green Belt policy on these lines has several advantages:

- it sustains the popular image of the Green Belt concept;

- it provides a coherent and consistent approach to development in the countryside;

- it provides the best chance for reducing the imbalanced provision for housing and employment generating developments within and beyond the Green Belt;

- it reduces the complexity and duplication which exists between several different restraint policies.

6

An Agenda for the Future

It is important to move from a moribund and outdated Green Belt policy to a more dynamic approach. In our view this new approach needs:

- to be supportive of existing regional development policy and urban regeneration goals;

- to be supportive of local planning policy in areas now outside the Green Belts and under enormous pressure for urban development of all kinds;

- to promote the improved use of open land and the quality of environment in the countryside.

One of the most important failings of present policy is its inability to steer development change at a regional scale (referred to in chapter 2). The Green Belt has had little direct bearing on the scale and spatial patterning of urban development - urban growth is allowed to take place in a largely random and incremental fashion resulting in a range of 'inefficiencies' brought about by leap-frogging over the Green Belts and the transfer of planning problems from one location to another.

GREEN AREAS RATHER THAN GREEN BELTS

We believe the concept of a 'belt' around a single city is redundant and should be replaced by that of a 'green area' around several cities, towns and villages. Much more extensive than the present Green Belts, this area could cover most of lowland rural England, with the exception of the conurbations and principal cities, Areas of Outstanding Natural Beauty and National Parks.

In order that Green Areas play a supportive and key role in regional development and urban regeneration at the national scale, they should be defined first in those regions under greatest pressure for countryside development - namely the South East, East Anglia, East and West Midlands, South West, North West and Yorkshire and Humberside. In the North of England and Scotland the scope for introducing Green Areas is less obvious given the more limited spatial extent of decentralised urban growth. There is already considerable flexibility in approach to countryside policy in Scotland and we see the case for a wider extension of the Dundee model.

The problem of defining Green Areas should be resolved in the context of the government's approach to regional strategic guidance, outlined in the recent White Paper.[66] Individual counties or groups of counties should define Green Areas in conjunction with the Department of Environment's regional offices during the process of identifying key issues and formulating strategic planning advice.[67] Separate central government advice would be necessary to ensure that all counties in the selected regions took steps to define Green Areas in line with national policy. Amended government advice could be contained in a reworked Planning Policy Guidance Note.

GREATER FLEXIBILITY

Important as the definition of Green Areas may be, it is just as crucial that they be seen as a policy device. Green Areas should be an effective mechanism for strategic management rather than, as in the case of National Parks, an end in their own right. For the general public and the developer a bewildering array of different planning policies apply in different areas; these need simplifying and co-ordinating. Often there is far too much detail, and this stifles initiative. Current Green Belt policy contains both broad policy objectives (to check the unrestricted sprawl of large built-up areas) as well as a set of detailed prescriptions for development change (i.e. what is and is not permitted). We think there is need to introduce greater flexibility into a Green Areas policy which should take the form of a set of strategic guidelines within which District authorities work, rather than a rigid set of development control criteria. This would leave the detailed planning control where it belongs, with the local authority, and it would allow greater scope for regional and local variation of interpretation.

GREEN AREA POLICY

The distinction between Green Belts and the ordinary countryside beyond Green Belts would disappear. There would no longer be a presumption against any new building. As with the present Green Belts, however, the aim would be that Green Areas should have a predominantly rural character. Because of the greater flexibility introduced by the Green Areas policy there would need to be some safeguards against developments which threaten the countryside. Need for development would be judged, as under present Green Belt or countryside policies, in relation to the damage it could do the rural appearance of the land. (Local authorities should insist that Environmental Impact Assessment procedures be used whenever practical.)

Because of the need to find alternative uses for farmland and buildings there is a case for giving agriculture and forestry greater consideration in planning, both in terms of the strategic options for locational change (e.g. new forests) and the inclusion of these uses within the category of 'development'. Public opposition is often voiced to farming change which damages the landscape and environment. At the same time the need to make changes in the use of agricultural land must be understood by local residents and politicians and by local planning and highway authorities. Amendments to the Use Classes Order could ensure a better balance between greater flexibility and more accountability in farming change.

Green Area policy would take the form of a set of criteria incorporated into the Structure Plans and used by the Districts as a set of guidelines when preparing Local Plans. Most Districts would be within designated Green Areas and they would be expected to make provision in their Green Areas for different kinds of urban development in line with strategic advice on levels of future housing and industrial change. But the application of Green Area policy would help secure the environmental protection of the countryside and the enhancement of the quality of the Green Areas. Examples of the kinds of criteria include:

- Separation of settlements: new development should not lead to the coalescence of larger and smaller cities and towns; very sensitive areas under pressure from urban development might be best protected by local authority ownership or open space use other than agriculture.

- Open land: zoning of land areas, especially for agricultural set-aside and forestry, should be encouraged provided it does not exclude mixed uses and uses which might change with fluctuations in agricultural or forestry policy.

- Tourism and recreation: informal and small-scale recreation and tourism facilities, especially small-scale holiday accommodation, should be encouraged.

- Degraded land: improvement of the quality of 'brownfield sites' between and within towns and cities should be promoted through recycling, reclamation of derelict and unused land; areas which can be developed with positive gains for the landscape setting.

- Housing: small sites for general housing provision should be provided in existing settlements with preference given to sites for local housing need where this can be demonstrated; sites would need to be identified which could be developed without detriment to the local environment and which, because of their proximity to existing built-up areas, could make use of existing infrastructure.

- Industry and commerce: expansion of small and medium-scale manufacturing enterprises but major retail developments confined to urban areas.

- New settlements: the development of new settlements planned within a regional context to take account of strategic housing requirements, the balance between existing and new settlements and the environmental impact of the policies.

THE NEXT STEPS

This report has emphasised the need to accommodate future urban growth within Green Areas. But how flexible should Green Areas be? How can the principles of the Green Area be introduced into Green Belts which are re-garded as permanent?

One positive outcome of the Working Party's studies would be for a small group to test the practicalities of rolling forward and implementing a Green Area policy using one or more case-study areas selected from within and without the present boundaries of the Green Belts. This could form part of a regional strategic planning exercise or be regarded as a project in its own right. The research would need to focus on the more dynamic parts of the outer metropolitan area presently untouched by Green Belts policy and in-clude a range of different local authorities, possibly in different regions. The research team would examine:

The scope for developing a national policy on Green Areas:

- relationships between Green Area policy and other State planning policies, existing and emerging;

- integration with other national policies, agriculture, transport, housing, rural enterprise, regional policy and the environment;

- the scope for amended policy guidance;

- the political acceptability of Green Area policy in terms of the interests of environmental organisations, developers and the general public.

The strategic role of Green Area policy:

- the need, if there is one, for definition of the boundaries of Green Areas;

- the relationship between Green Area policy and the future scale of development in the countryside - especially levels of future housing and employment;

- the nature and effectiveness of regional strategic guidance and County Policy Statements.

The implementation of Green Area policy in the context of the proposed changes in the development planning system:

- the inclusion of Green Areas in District-wide Local Plans especially policies for different parts of the Green Areas, for example in terms of land use or environmental quality;

- the flexibility to be built in to the policy, frequency of review and extent of change proposed by a review;

- the relationship between the existing initiatives pursued by local authorities, Groundwork Trusts and the type of approaches and their possible co-ordination with Green Area guidelines.

The research should be funded by as wide a partnership of interests as possible, drawing on the resources of:

- central government, especially the Department of the Environment;

- local authorities, a group of Counties and Districts;

- environmental interests - the Council for the Protection of Rural England for example;

- private sector - the Housebuilders Federation for example.

Green Belts have become an outmoded and largely irrelevant mechanism for handling the complexity of future change in the city's countryside. If abandoned they should be replaced by a more robust policy which meets the growing concerns of the 'green' movement and provides a more efficient framework than presently exists for the operation of market forces.

In our view the question of the future of Green Belts is intimately related to that of the planning system. If Green Area policy is to become a reality the government will need to strengthen the planning system to ensure that the environment will be protected. Stronger land-use planning would in our opinion be consistent with the growing political salience of 'green' issues reflected by the government's stated desire for greater controls over farming and the 'greening' of business activity recently announced by Lord Young.[68]

The element of strategic land management implied by this report may well provide the greater certainty and co-ordination desired by groups like the Confederation of British Industry and the Housebuilders Federation on the one hand and the Council for the Protection of Rural England on the other hand.

References

1. Department of Environment (January 1988), Planning Policy Guidance Note 2.

2. Scottish Development Department (1985), 'Development in the Countryside and Green Belts', Circular 24/85, para 2.

3. Town and Country Planning Association (1986), 'Dispersal: A Call for Action' in Martin Elson, *Green Belts: Conflict Mediation in the Urban Fringe*, London, Heinemann.

4. Ministry of Housing and Local Government (1962), *Green Belts*, London, HMSO.

5. S. Fothergill (1986), 'Industrial employment and planning restraint in the London Green Belt'; paper given at Kingston Polytechnic, 11 April 1986, Mimeo.

6. An ARC report estimates the Green Belt has cost £14.6 billion, *Financial Times*, 23 January, 1988.

7. D. White (1985), 'What Green Belts are for?', *New Society*, 17 January, 85-89.

8. D. Lock (1988), 'Green Belts and the direction of urban development'; paper given at the Landscape Institute/Royal Town Planning Institute conference 'Green Belts and City - Poverty or Pleasure?', 12th May.

9. D. L. Saunders (1977), 'The changing planning framework' in F. Joyce (ed.), *Metropolitan Development and Change. The West Midlands: a policy review*, Saxon House.

10. D. Lock, *op. cit.*

11. This point is confirmed by the research carried out by A. Champion, K. Clegg and R. L. Davies (1977), *Facts about the New Towns: a socio-economic digest*. Newcastle, Retailing and Planning Associates.

12. J. Young (1988), 'Is this the Green Belt buckling?' *The Times*, 20th May.

13. Scottish Development Department, *op. cit.*

14. Lord Elton (1986), *Estates Times*, May 23rd.

15. See for instance C. M. Harrison (1981), 'A playground for whom? Informal recreation in London's Green Belt', *Area*, 13, 109-114.

16. Quoted in D. White, *op. cit.*

17. Polly Toynbee (1988), 'A fragile ring', *The Guardian*, 28th May.

18. D. G. Gregory (1970), *Green Belts and development control: a case study of the West Midlands.* Occasional Paper No. 12, University of Birmingham, Centre for Urban and Regional Studies.

19. Research carried out by Steven Molnar (1986), 'Green Belt policy and the countryside', submitted to the Working Party.

20. Polly Toynbee, *op. cit.*

21. R. S. Horsman (1988), 'Shades of Green', Department of Environment representative, paper to the Landscape Institute/Royal Town Planning Institute, *Green Belts and City - Poverty or Pleasure?*, 12th May.

22. David Lock, *op. cit.*

23. Department of Environment (1988), *The Green Belts*. London, HMSO.

24. Scottish Development Department, *op. cit.*

25. Department of Environment (1980), 'Development Control - Policy and Practice', Circular 22/80, para 4 (Circular 40/80, Welsh Office).

26. House of Commons Environment Committee (1984), *Green Belts and Land for Housing*, vols. 267-275

27. Planning permission for the 'Golden Triangle' site near the M1/M25 junction at Bricket Wood, Hertfordshire was refused by the Secretary of State following a planning appeal - costs were awarded against the developers - reported in *Journal of Planning and Environmental Law*, Bulletin, April 1989, 2-3.

28. Department of Environment (1989), *The Future of Development Plans*, London, HMSO.

29. West Midlands Forum of County Councils (1986), West Midlands Regional Strategy Review. Background Report: no. 5, *The Green Belt*, 1.

30. *Ibid.*

31. Chester City Council's Local Plan sought to remove 200 acres, reported in *The Planner* (1988), vol. 74, no. 11. Following a Public Local Inquiry the Inspector rejected this proposal, reported in *Planning*, vol. 812, 31 March 1989.

32. Martin Simmons (1988), 'Keeping the Green Belt up-to-date: the case of North West Kent', *The Planner*, 74, 5, 13-16.

33. Association of Municipal Authorities (1985), *Green Policy: a review of green policy and practice in metropolitan authorities*, London, AMA.

34. Lothian Regional Council (1983), *Green Belt Agreement*, LRC.

35. Strathclyde Regional Council (1987), Clyde Calders Executive Group - Calders Urban Fringe Management Project; First Annual Report 1983-84; Fourth Annual Report 1986-7.

36. Adam Smith Institute (1988), *The Green Quadratic*, 5. ASI.

37. John Newman (1988), 'Green Belt retailing - a developer's view'; paper given to the Landscape Institute/Royal Town Planning Institute conference, 5th May.

38. See, for instance, evidence from the House Builders Federation to the Department of Environment Inquiry into British Housing (1985), January.

39. Comment based on research carried out by Steven Molnar, *op. cit.*

40. The processes of urban dispersal are fully discussed by John Herington (1984), *The Outer City*, London, Paul Chapman Ltd.

41. John Herington (1984), 'Green Belt red herring', *Town and Country Planning*, vol. 53, no. 3, March.

42. See, for instance, P. Jones (1986), 'Scotland's urban fringes', *The Planner*, vol. 72 (8), 12-14; and R. Dent (1979), 'Green Belt planning in Strathkelvin', Proceedings of Planning Exchange Conference.

43. R. D. Beaumont (1988), 'Glasgow city region - case study on Green Belts'.

44. Action with Communities in Rural England (ACRE) (1988), *Who Can Afford to Live in the Countryside?* and *Affordable Homes in the Countryside? A role for private builders?*, Fairford, ACRE.

45. Department of Environment (1988), *Housing in Rural Areas: Village Housing and New Villages: a discussion paper*. July.

46. Department of Environment News Release 63, 3.2.89, *Low Cost Housing in Rural Areas*; and Department of Environment News Release 64, 3.2.89, *Low Cost Housing Needs in Rural Areas*.

47. Department of Environment (1988), *Rural Enterprise and Development*, Planning Policy Guidance 7, London, HMSO.

48. John Billingham (1989), 'Seeking solutions at rural pressure points', *Planning*, vol. 814, 14th April.

49. Chris Amos (1989), 'A testing time for new settlements?' *Town and Country Planning*, vol. 58, no. 11, November.

50. Reported in *The Guardian*, 11th March, 1988.

51. House of Commons Environment Committee (1984), *First Report from the Environment Committee, Green Belts and Land for Housing*, Session 83-84 vol. 1, p. xx.

52. T. Cherrett (1982), *The Implementation of Green Belt Policy*. Gloucestershire Papers in Local and Rural planning no. 15, 5-35, GCAT.

53. Edgar A. Rose and Gordon E. Cherry (1986), 'New approaches to the twenty-first century city', a paper for the Department of Environment, West Midlands Regional Office. Centre for Urban and Regional Studies, University of Birmingham.

54. G. Collins (1988), 'Policies and design in the Green Belt', papers to the Landscape Institute/RTPI conference, 12th May.

55. S. Clifford (1988), 'Ideas on the fringe: people and places not policies', paper to the Landscape Institute/RTPI conference, 12th May.

56. E. Grice (1988), 'Anywhere else - but not in my backyard', *Sunday Times*, 15th May; see also, S. Barwick (1988), 'Ridley opposed homes near his own', *The Independent*, 15th June.

57. Department of Environment (1988), *The Green Belts, op. cit.*, 33.

58. House of Commons Environment Committee, *op. cit.*, para 13, xiv.

59. *Ibid.*, xiii.

60. Strathclyde Regional Council (1986), *Structure Plan 1981*, Update, SRC.

61. P. Hall (1989), *London 2001*, London, Unwin Hyman.

62. Royal Town Planning Institute (1986), *The Challenge of Change*, London, RTPI.

63. Nuffield Foundation (1986), *Town and Country Planning - A Report to the Nuffield Foundation*, London, Nuffield.

64. David Lock (1989), *Riding the Tiger: Planning the South of England - a discussion paper*, Town and Country Planning Association, London.

65. Richard Munton (1983), *London's Green Belt: Containment in Practice*, London, Allen and Unwin.

66. Department of Environment (1989), *The Future of Development Plans*, *op. cit.*

67. Strategic regional planning is further encouraged by Mr Patten's recent statement outlined in Department of Environment (1989), *Structure Plans and Regional Planning Guidance*.

68. Reported in *The Times*, 11th May, 1989.

Appendix I

Great Britain Land Area statistics including Green Belts

Land Area of:

Scotland	7,878,337 ha
England and Wales	17,197,586 ha

Urban Area of:

Scotland	237,000 ha
England and Wales	1,891,734 ha

Urban Area as a Percentage of Land Area

Scotland	3%
England and Wales	11%

Green Belt

Scotland (1988)	135,930 ha
England and Wales* (1986)	1,821,862 ha
Scotland (1979)	218,470 ha
England and Wales* (1979)	679,000 ha

Green Belt as a Percentage of Land Area

Scotland (1988)	1.72%
England and Wales* (1986)	12.10%
Scotland (1979)	2.77%
England and Wales* (1979)	4.51%

Green Belts in Scotland

Lothian	14,600 ha
Aberdeen	15,000 ha
Greater Glasgow	100,000 ha
Falkirk/Grangemouth	3,495 ha
Ayr/Prestwick	2,835 ha
Total	135,930 ha
Dundee Countryside Policy Area	14,800 ha

*There are no Green Belts in Wales

Sources
Green Belts, Martin J Elson, Heinemann, London, 1986
Scottish Abstract of Statistics, Scottish Office, 1987
Land Use summary Sheet No 4, Revised 1981

Appendix II

Approved Green Belts in England

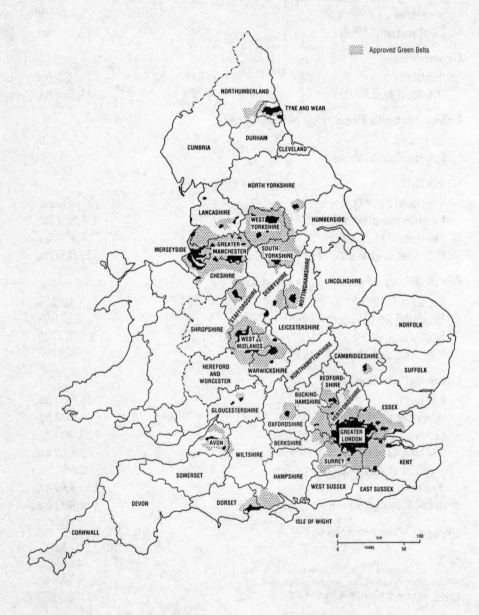

Approved Green Belts

NORTHUMBERLAND

TYNE AND WEAR

CUMBRIA

DURHAM

CLEVELAND

NORTH YORKSHIRE

LANCASHIRE

WEST YORKSHIRE

HUMBERSIDE

MERSEYSIDE

GREATER MANCHESTER

SOUTH YORKSHIRE

CHESHIRE

DERBYSHIRE

NOTTINGHAMSHIRE

LINCOLNSHIRE

STAFFORDSHIRE

SHROPSHIRE

LEICESTERSHIRE

NORFOLK

WEST MIDLANDS

HEREFORD AND WORCESTER

WARWICKSHIRE

NORTHAMPTONSHIRE

CAMBRIDGESHIRE

SUFFOLK

BEDFORD-SHIRE

BUCKING-HAMSHIRE

HERTFORDSHIRE

ESSEX

GLOUCESTERSHIRE

OXFORDSHIRE

GREATER LONDON

AVON

BERKSHIRE

KENT

WILTSHIRE

SURREY

SOMERSET

HAMPSHIRE

WEST SUSSEX

EAST SUSSEX

DEVON

DORSET

ISLE OF WIGHT

CORNWALL

km 0 100
miles 0 50